Career Readiness

for Teens

1 2 3 4 5

S T A R T

Chad Foster

ISBN: 0-9644456-6-6

Printed in the United States of America

Cover Design by Madison Studios
www.madisonstudios.com

Text Editing by Dana Buxton
danabuxton@gmail.com

Text Design by Kristen James
kristen@bravadopublishing.com

Dedication

To our sons, Graham and Mason, who are two of the greatest gifts that God has ever sent my way. I love both of you more than you will ever know.

Contents

Career

An occupation undertaken for a significant period of a person's life.

Readiness

The state of being fully prepared for something.

Ready or Not?

How could anyone in his right mind want to write a book about work? I mean it's painful enough for most people to even think about and/or talk about work. But should you really have to read a book on the subject of *work*? At least for the next few minutes, trust me on this one. You need to know what it takes to be ready for the world of work.

Most employers today are very critical of young workers. These employers say that the vast majority of young people have very little work ethic and lack fundamental workplace skills. They say that too many young people are not *career ready*. Business owners go on and on about how much young people don't know when it comes to the world of work.

Is that a fair description of the average young worker? Maybe yes…maybe no. But, what if it is true? What if those business owners are correct when they say young people are clueless when it comes to the world of work? And what if this has been going on for years and years? And, if it is true, who's to blame?

If the employers are right, and they might be, then you should be celebrating right now. You should be excited to hear that news. You should be thankful that it is what it is because that means your generation has an incredible opportunity to be much more successful than all other generations before you. Here's why.

What if you moved to a new town the summer before your freshman year of high school and you really wanted to play on the basketball team at your new school? And, what if you were the only freshman trying out for a team that had nine other players on it who were all juniors and seniors? And, what if your junior and senior teammates had decent basketball skills, but nothing special? What if they could shoot, dribble, jump, and run pretty well...but none of them were very good passers? I mean they couldn't make a decent pass if their lives depended on it.

Are you still with me here? Are you wondering how this could happen? It happens all the time, so hang in there with me for a minute.

This could easily happen if the coach that your teammates had in middle school didn't spend enough time helping his players develop good passing skills *before* they entered high school? The coach made them work on dribbling, shooting, and rebounding, but they never got around to practicing their passing skills. So, as you might imagine, their passing skills didn't improve much. In fact, their passing skills were pitiful.

Fortunately, you did practice your passing skills in middle school, and you became an excellent passer.

How did that happen?

Remember, you just moved to this new town, and you went to a different middle school than your older teammates. And, luckily, your middle school coach knew how important it would be for you to develop and practice all skills, including passing skills, *before* you entered high school. Your coach also knew that most middle school coaches were not making passing skills a priority for their players. So, your middle school coach added two plus two and came up with four! Bingo!

Your middle school coach prepared you for high school basketball with a set of skills that most others didn't possess. You arrived at high school with great passing skills.

Bottom line...you had one critical basketball skill that your older teammates did not have. So, when the season started and *game time* arrived, you were an invaluable asset to the team even though you were just a freshman. You were more prepared with more skills than your older teammate were so, while you played, they sat on the bench and watched. In this case, they were not *game-ready*.

It will be exactly this way when you enter the world of work. I didn't say *if* you enter the world of work. I said *when* you enter the world of work. You see, this one's not optional. At some point, every student's educational journey comes to an end, and they enter the workforce. When they get there, some are career ready and some are not. Those who are fully prepared have an incredible head start over those who are not.

It does not matter how old you are when you enter the world of work. And it does not matter in which city or town you grow up. Nor does it matter what color your skin is or who your parents might be.

The bottom line is pretty simple. We all eventually end up in the workplace, and when we get there, we are either career ready or we are not. If we are really and truly ready to perform at our chosen career, then our chances of success are very good. If we show up in the real world of work and we are not ready, someone else will enjoy the success we could, and should, have had.

You might not know this, but 20 years ago this was not the way things were in the world of work. My parents, like many of your parents, were able to get jobs pretty easily if they had received a good education. There were plenty of jobs to go around, and almost everyone who wanted a job could get one. And, when our parents got their jobs, most of them had a chance to develop their workplace skills *after* they started working. Twenty years ago it was not that important to enter the world of work already career ready. Today it is essential.

Why is that the way it is now?

Well, things have changed a great deal over the past 20 years. Today, there are not enough jobs to go around, so many people are unemployed. The competition for jobs is much greater today than it was in the past. Remember the junior and senior basketball players who did not have all the skills they needed to succeed? They could run, dribble, jump, and shoot, but they could not pass? Even as a freshman, you were game-ready with a full set of skills that gave you a clear advantage over many of the upper classmen on your team.

That means if you do the work now, while you are still in school, and commit to being career ready before you hit the world of work, then you will be one of those young people who has a great chance to succeed. You will have an advantage. You will have a head start in the real-world race, and a head start in any race is always a good thing.

Pretty simple formula, don't you think?

Notes

The Whole Truth

Several years ago, I was in the business of building tennis courts and running tracks. One day I came up with an idea to use recycled tire rubber to create a soft, safe playground surface that kids could fall on without busting their heads wide open. Lucky for our company, McDonald's and Disney decided to use the new product on their playgrounds around the world. In fact, we installed our SAF DEK surface on more than 3,000 McDonald's Playlands. Our company was eventually sold, and I decided to take some time off to do something I had wanted to do for a long time…travel. I wanted to travel across America to see what there was to see and to learn what I could learn. So I did. I packed up my belongings, jumped into my old Ford Explorer, and hit the road.

I did see and I did learn a great deal as I traveled. Along the way, I also got pretty angry about what I was seeing and what I was learning.

There are many great things about traveling across the country, but for me, the people I met as I traveled were the highlight of the trip. By the way, this was no short trip we're talking about here. What I thought was going to be a nice relaxing three-month cross-country trip ended up being a two-year journey that took me to and through 40 different states! That means I probably traveled right through the state in which you live and maybe even stopped in your hometown. That's 730 straight days in an old Ford Explorer, all alone. No dog, no best friend, no girlfriend, no iPod, iPad, or even iPhone! Hard to imagine, I'm sure, but that's the way it was back then.

Remember I told you that, as I traveled, I did get pretty ticked off along the way. Why would anyone taking a two-year vacation get ticked off? Very simple. As I traveled, it became more and more apparent to me that young people like you were only getting half of what you bargained for when you agreed to come to school, sit in class, do your homework, and take your tests. Most of you are in the midst of getting a good education, which is great. However, very few of you are getting the full preparation you will need to be successful in the world of work! You are not being fully prepared for your inevitable destination after you complete your educational journey.

It's not the fault of your teachers or your principals or even your parents. It just is the way it is, but it's not right and it's not fair to you and all of your classmates.

Here's what I saw as I made my way across this great country.

Everywhere I stopped along the way I met new people. People I had never met before. People I knew nothing about. Young people, old people...people from all walks of life. Rich people, poor people...all kinds of people. Tall people, short people...you name it, I met them. I can't remember all of the people I met along the way. I wish I could remember them all, but can you imagine how many people you can meet in 730 days??

Obviously, I can't remember them all, yet there were some people I will never forget. That's because when I met these particular people and heard their stories I got more and more frustrated. The people I am talking about were all young people, most of them in their early 20s, and many of them were about to graduate from college.

Isn't that great…about to graduate from college! Just what we keep encouraging all of you to do. Graduate from high school and then continue your education. Go to college and get a degree. That's all fine and well, but the truth of the matter is that every one of you will need more than just that college degree if you really want to succeed in the real world.

If we fail to make sure you understand this and if we don't tell you the *rest of the story*, then we have done a great disservice to you and to all of your classmates. We owe you the whole truth, and many of the young people I met as I traveled cross-country weren't quite getting that whole truth.

Somehow these soon-to-be college graduates thought they would be able to trade their college degree for a great job and a successful career. They were of the opinion that a good education was all they needed. However, as they got closer and closer to graduating, they began to realize that something was missing. As they started the process of trying to figure out what they would do *after* they got their degrees, many of them came to the same conclusion. Yes, they were educated, but no, they were not really prepared for their future careers.

So, day after day, week after week, I ran into bright, well-educated young people who were all trying to figure out what to do with the rest of their lives. When asked, almost 80% of them said that they had no idea what they wanted to do when they completed their educational journey, and almost all of them were scared. That's why I ended my two-year, 40-state journey in such a state of frustration.

Let me see if I have this right. When you were a little kid, we told you how important it was to get a good education. If you had the nerve to ask why, which is definitely a fair question, you were probably told that you would need a good education in order to get a good job when you left the four walls of the classroom and entered the world of work. So far…so good. But that's where we dropped the ball. That's where we let you down. In fact, that's where we forgot to tell you the whole story. Furthermore, that's why, if you are not careful, you might end up in the same boat as all of those confused, scared young people I met on my cross-country journey.

If you ever have to testify in a court of law, before you take your place on the witness stand, the court clerk will ask you to raise your right hand; then, he or she will ask you if you "swear to tell the truth, the whole truth, and nothing but the truth, so help you God?" When you agree to do that, the whole world expects you to live up to that promise you just made. In court, if you don't tell the whole truth, the judge can actually hold you in contempt and put your rear end in jail! That's why it's so important to get the whole truth because if you only get part of the truth you won't have all the information you need to make the right decisions and choices about your future.

Getting only part of the truth is probably what happened to most of you when you walked into school for the very first time. You were told that you would need a good education in order to succeed later in life. That was, and is, still true. But that wasn't the whole truth. That was just part of the truth, and part of the truth is not what you deserve. You deserve the whole truth, and here's why.

If you start in first grade and continue your educational journey all the way through college, you will spend approximately 20,000 hours in a classroom. That's 20,000 hours of your valuable time. If you waste any part of that 20,000 hours, then shame on you. If we help you waste any of that 20,000 hours, then shame on us.

In my opinion, if you are going to invest that kind of time and effort in your future, you deserve to know what else you will need, beyond a good education, to succeed at your inevitable destination – the world of work. It's just like those great young people I met on my cross-country trip several years ago. Yes, they were *educated*; unfortunately, somewhere along the way, we forgot to fully *prepare* them. The whole truth is that education and preparation are both critical to success in the world of work.

That word *success* will pop up several times in this book, so perhaps this is a good time to consider an appropriate definition for the word success. Just stop for a minute and think about your definition of the word success.

What does success mean to you?

Think about a few people in your life who you would describe as successful. Why do you consider them successful? Is it because of something they have? Or maybe something they did? Or maybe even something in which they believe?

That's how I once defined success...money, fame, stuff...but not anymore. Now, after meeting thousands of so-called successful people, I have a new definition for success. Most people take too long to figure this one out, but those who figure it out early are the lucky ones.

Success, in my opinion, is about four things – good friends, a good reputation, career satisfaction, and helping others. Despite being a pretty simple definition, it is often much easier to say than it is to practice. Just give it some thought before you get too far down the road.

Whatever you do, please remember this: Success has nothing to do with money! Money cannot, does not, will not, and has not *ever* made anyone happy. Now, don't misunderstand me here. There is nothing wrong with money. I like money, but money can't make you happy. In fact, I have more miserable rich friends than I could ever count. So, before you start making plans and setting goals, spend a little time coming up with your own good definition for success.

As you know, the workplace is where you and all of your classmates are headed. And, as you know, along the way you will spend approximately 20,000 hours in a classroom. You probably think that's a long time and a whole bunch of hours. I would agree.

If you think 20,000 hours in a classroom is unbelievable, take a guess as to how many hours most of you will spend in the world of work. Get ready for this one because it can make you dizzy when you first hear it. Most of you will spend approximately 86,000 hours of your life at work. No kidding...true story! So I'm thinking if we know that the workplace is where all of you will end up, and we also know that you will be there for 86,000 hours, the least we can do is help prepare you for that rather extended experience.

Everyone eventually chooses a career and goes to work. Some go after college. Some go after high school. Some go even earlier than that. But sooner or later, we all go to work. This book is all about work...how, when, where, why, and with whom you will work. This book is also about what we owe you as a student who is in the process of investing 20,000 hours of your valuable time as you get ready to enter the 86,000-hour world of work.

Remember, it's your 86,000 hours, and you're either going to enjoy the ride or it's going to wear you out. Fortunately, you get to choose which it will be.

Notes

The Quiz

Work: Physical or mental activity directed toward the production or accomplishment of something.

Work is work, whether it's a part-time job you have as a teen or a full-time job you land when your educational journey is over. The rules of the game don't change, and the results of your efforts don't either. Since I mentioned part-time work, this might be a good time to inform you that there is a strong correlation, or relationship, between part-time work as a teen and success later in life as a full-time worker. In fact, the *number one* common denominator among successful people across this country is part-time work as a teenager.

The number one common denominator among successful people is *not* earning straight **A**'s in school or even super high SAT scores. Now don't misunderstand me. There is nothing wrong with straight **A**'s and high SAT scores. Both are great to have and will certainly be helpful along the way, but the number one common denominator among successful people is, and probably always will be, part-time work as a teen.

Why is that true?

It's true because during your part-time work experience you will learn and have a chance to practice the same skills that will be needed for success in your full-time careers later in life. It doesn't matter if you end up working in a blue-collar job, a white-collar job, or any color job on earth. And it won't matter if you end up working in a big city, in a small town, or somewhere in-between. The workplace skills you develop (learn) and use (practice) as a part-time worker will be critical to your future success.

Why is this true? Since I have a pretty simple mind, I'll give you a pretty simple answer.

When you get your first full-time job, the <u>knowledge</u> you acquired during your 20,000 hour educational journey will help you *understand* your job. On the other hand, the <u>skills</u> you acquire during your part-time work experience will help you actually *do* your job. How well you *understand* the job is only part of the process, and it's not the biggest part. How well you *do* your job, day after day, week after week, month after month, and year after year is the key that will unlock the doors to success for you and for all of your classmates.

This will hold true for all jobs and all careers. Speaking of jobs and careers, now might be a good time to discuss the difference between the two. Let's say that you decide to pursue a career in teaching. A very respected career for sure. Within the teaching career, there are numerous possible jobs that you might have. For instance, you might be a middle school math teacher for a few years and later switch to teaching science in high school. Most people assume that they will have several different jobs over time, but very few people realize that they will also have a multitude of *careers* as well. In fact, current statistics tell us that most of you will change careers, not just jobs but careers, 7-8 times over the course of your lives. Think about that. Can you imagine having seven or even eight different careers? I have already had eight careers of my own, and I might even have a few more.

Get ready because that's the way it's going to be for you and all of your friends--lots of job and career changes along the way as you navigate your way through your 86,000-hour real-world journey. Wouldn't it be nice to have a solid set of skills that could move with you from job to job and career to career?

As a part-time worker (paid or unpaid), you will have multiple opportunities to learn, develop, and improve your *workplace skills*. And, since workplace skills are like all skills, whether it's riding a bike, driving a car, or playing a piano, we know that once you learn them you never forget them. The same workplace skills will apply to each and every job and/or career you pursue. That is huge for you since you will be making so many job and career changes along the way. The secret is to enter the real world with a set of skills that will work for you regardless of where you end up working and regardless of how many times you change jobs and/or careers.

We know something else about these workplace skills. Like all skills, they must be learned, and they only improve if and when they are practiced. We also know that most skills can be learned at an early age, so it's never too early to start learning them. The earlier you learn workplace skills the better off you will be since learning them early gives you more time to practice, and ultimately improve, those skills.

Think about the first time you tried to ride a bike...after the training wheels came off. You got up on that bike and off you went...literally! You fell on your butt so many times you lost count. Maybe you went six feet before you fell or maybe you even made it ten feet, but eventually you came crashing down. And it happened time after time after time...until one day...the handle bars didn't wobble, you didn't lean too far over to one side, your foot didn't slip off the pedal, and somehow you finally got it. That bike cruised down the street with you mounted on top and a great big smile planted on your face as your mom or dad ran alongside, cheering you on.

You had learned a new skill. You could ride a bike.

Never mind the fact that since you had never ridden more than 10 feet before falling, you had also never learned how to properly stop or turn the bike. So, it happened again. Your stopping and turning skills were non-existent and down you went...one more time...flat on your cute little face. Some of you might even have a scar to help you remember those face-plants you experienced as a kid. Now you know why the person who invented the bike helmet is so filthy rich!

The point is that you only know how to ride a bike today because you *learned* the skill of bike riding many years ago, and that skill only improved as you continued to *practice* it over time. Most important, you still possess that skill, and even if you don't ride your bike for 99 days, you could still jump on that bike on day 100 and ride again. Once you have the skill, you will always have the skill, and that's the way it goes with all skills, even *workplace skills*.

But what about all that knowledge everyone keeps telling you is so important? What about all those facts and figures you have to memorize and then regurgitate (big word for puke) at test time? What about that legitimate question you want to ask almost every day: "Why do I have to learn this stuff?" Remember the story about the court clerk asking the witness if they "swear to tell the whole truth, nothing but the truth...?" Well, here we go again.

The whole truth is that some of the *stuff* you are being asked to memorize in class will never be needed except on that painful day when you will be asked to spit the info back up for a test.

Yes, it is true that you are going to be asked to memorize many bits of knowledge that you will probably never need to know in order to effectively do your job in your chosen career(s). It happened to me, it will happen to you, and it will keep on happening for many years to come.

For instance, can you remember which part of the human cell provides the energy? Or, do you know what year the Wright

Brothers made their inaugural flight? How about who won the Battle of Mt. Roaring in World War II?

How did you do on that little quiz? Anyone make a 100%? I doubt it.

Most of us, included yours truly, were taught the answer to question #1 before we reached high school. We were also taught the answer to question #2 during elementary school. However, the truth of the matter is that 90% of adults, including myself, can't remember the correct answers to questions #1 and #2 because we never really *learned* that information. We simply memorized the information, spit it back out for the test, and then proceeded to forget it. If we had truly learned the information we would be able to recall it now.

Here's a perfect example. Can you tell me on what date you were born? Of course you can! Bet you got that one right, didn't you? See, now we are talking about knowledge that you found *relevant*. It has real meaning to you, so you will never forget it. That's why it is so important for us to do everything in our power to make sure that what you are being asked to learn is relevant.

By the way, don't feel bad if you flunked that little 3-question quiz I just asked you to take. I have given that quiz to more than 5,000 teachers and principals, and 90% of them flunked it as well...90%!

Just for fun go ahead and try it out on a few of your teachers. Ask them to take the 3-question quiz. They are definitely a group of well-educated people. See how they do; then, after they flunk the quiz, ask them this question: "Can you effectively do your current job without being able to correctly answer those quiz questions?" Finally, ask them the even more important question: "If you did need that knowledge to effectively do your job, but you *didn't* have the knowledge, how long would it take you to access the knowledge?" Weeks? Days? Hours?

Can you spell Google?? The correct answer is *minutes*, or maybe even seconds! That knowledge, like almost all knowledge, can easily be accessed in a matter of minutes if needed,

The bottom line is quite simple. In today's workplace environment, *having* the knowledge is not always as important as being able to *access* the knowledge. Fortunately, you and your friends are very good at accessing knowledge. In fact, there has never been a more talented generation than yours at accessing knowledge. Isn't that true?

By the way, if you got question #3 about the Battle of Mt. Roaring correct, you are in a very special group of people. You are also in a very small group of people.

That group would be the group of incredible liars since there is no correct answer to question #3! There was never any Battle of Mt. Roaring in World War II, or any other war for that matter. I totally made that up just to see if we had any truth-stretchers reading this book! I chose the word Roaring because it rhymes with "boring," a word many of you correctly use when you are asked to learn stuff you know you don't need to know.

So, what's the point? Give me a minute. I am almost there.

When we start to consider what information we are going to ask you to learn in class, it is critically important that we do our best to be sure that the knowledge we ask you to learn is, in fact, relevant. There is not enough time, not even 20,000 hours, to provide you with 100% of all knowledge. We all know that. So what knowledge is most relevant? That's the $100,000 question.

I am not qualified to answer that question. It's up to people who are much smarter than I am to decide what knowledge is most relevant for you. What I do know is that if we are going to fully prepare *and* educate you and your classmates we are going to have to find a healthy balance between the knowledge we ask you to acquire and the skills we know you will need in order to succeed in the real world.

Get ready. Here comes the point I've been promising.

We've already talked about knowledge that may or may not be relevant and how easily it can be accessed if and when it is needed. Now, go back to your teachers and/or parents and find out what percentage of them have jobs that require communication skills, people skills, time-management skills, technology skills, critical-thinking skills, and problem-solving skills to do their current jobs effectively.

If they are honest, the answer will be pretty close to 100%. In fact, just about every job in the world requires the skills I just listed.

So, what will happen to people who need, but don't have, these workplace skills when they arrive at their jobs? What are they going to do if they don't have the communication skills, technology skills, people skills, time-management skills, critical-thinking, and problem-solving skills that you now know are essential for success in all jobs?

We have established that they won't be able to do their jobs effectively without these skills. So, are they going to be in big trouble without these skills? Are their jobs at risk? Is there a chance they could lose their jobs just because they don't have these critical workplace skills?

Yes, their jobs are at risk. Yes, there is a good chance that they could lose their jobs. And yes, they are definitely in big trouble.

Why?

Here comes another simple answer from my very simple mind. They are in big trouble because, even if they can spell Google, this time it won't be of any help to them. Without these critical skills, they will struggle because, while they may be able to pull up Google and instantly access all kinds of valuable knowledge, they can't just type *communication skills* in the Google bar and instantly be great communicators. And you can't Google *problem solving skills* and suddenly start solving problems left and right!

Hopefully, that makes sense to you. Skills are skills, and they must be learned by doing, not by Googling (is that a word?). And skills only improve when they are practiced, not when they are Googled!

Remember the story about learning to ride a bike? It doesn't matter if we are talking about riding a bike or communicating, shooting a basketball or problem-solving, playing a piano or networking. The facts don't change.

1. **Skills must be learned.**

2. **Skills can be learned at an early age.**

3. **Skills only improve when they are practiced.**

No skills...no chance of being career ready... and no way you will succeed.

So, bottom line...when you get that first job in the real world, where you will definitely need all of those workplace skills, you better have the skills on arrival and you better have practiced them so that they will have time to improve as much as possible.

KNOWLEDGE QUIZ

Get out your iPads and/or smart phones and see how long it takes you to find the answers to these four questions. Google away and see how quickly you complete the quiz.

1. What is the square root of pi?

2. Who was the 33rd US President?

3. How many teeth should an adult have?

4. Who wrote the *Adventures of Huckleberry Finn,* and when was he born?

How did it go? Pretty quick I bet. In today's world, knowledge is extremely accessible, isn't it?

Just curious…how long do you think it might take you to learn a skill like juggling?

Go ahead, try to Google that one!

Notes

The Thief

When I was 13…and it's none of your business how long ago that might have been…I got a job. Not a full-time job because, obviously, I was in school at that time – eighth grade to be exact. But after school, almost every day of the week and for sure on Saturdays, I worked at a store that sold tennis equipment, clothes, shoes, etc. It wasn't a big store. In fact, there were only two other people working at the store. There was the guy who owned the store, Mr. Regan, and one other employee. Her name was Becky, and I will never forget that girl. I will never forget Becky because she changed my life and provided me with an amazing opportunity that opened the door to success for me. Remember, I was 13 years old at the time. Yes, it can happen when you are just a teenager!

The tennis store was close to where I lived, so I rode my bike to work each day after school. Mr. Regan hired me to work in his store because he knew I loved to play tennis. He was also

25

keenly aware that I knew anyone and everyone who played tennis in our little town. He also gave me the job because I walked into his store and asked for it.

There is no way you will get many *Yes* answers in life if you are not willing to ask. Sure, you will get your fair share of *No's* as well, but that's just part of the process. In fact, it is a very important part of the process. If you can learn now, at an early age, how to deal with the *No's* in life, you will have one more advantage over most people, many of whom never figure this out.

Back to my first part-time job and my co-worker, Becky. There are a couple of reasons why that seemingly insignificant part-time job, at age 13, opened the door to success for me.

First, working in a tennis shop gave me an opportunity to work in an environment that was related to something for which I had great passion. Tennis was indeed my passion, and that made coming to work every day seem like anything but work.

Ever thought about what your passion might be? You can be sure that your passion is related to one or more of your natural talents. Everyone has natural talents, even you!

Pay close attention to yourself and your interests, and see if you can figure out what your passion(s) might be. If you are one of the fortunate people who lands a job related to your passion, you might go all the way through life and never even think of your job as work. Now, wouldn't that be sweet?

Second, I lucked out when I went to work for Mr. Regan. I really did luck out because Mr. Regan didn't only want me to *work* for him. He also wanted me to *learn* from him. He was a successful businessman who was determined to teach me more than the average teenage employee was supposed to learn at a part-time job. Yes, there are adults out there like that. Adults who are interested in helping you prepare for your entry into the real world. Those people are definitely out there. However, they probably won't come knocking on your door, so be on the lookout.

Why Mr. Regan felt the way he did I will never know for sure, but for me, it all started right there in that tennis shop in a small town in Louisiana when I was 13 years old. The process of succeeding in life does not start the day you graduate from high school or even college. It starts long before that, and the earlier you start, the better your chances will be. Don't be like all those young people I met as I traveled across America on my two-year journey. They waited too long to start preparing to succeed. You can do better. Success can start today for every one of you.

Starting with my first day on the job, Mr. Regan taught me everything he possibly could about his business. He taught me how to string tennis rackets and how to sell shoes and tennis equipment. He taught me how to deal with customers, even the difficult ones. He also taught me to remember all of the customers' names so that I could call them by their name when they came into the store. People really seemed to like that. He even taught me how to order and manage inventory in the store and how to advertise and market our products.

Mr. Regan taught me most of the workplace skills I know today. I was only 13 when that happened. At the risk of repeating myself, I will say that one more time.

I was only 13 when I learned most of the workplace skills I have today. It's never too early to learn those skills.

That's right. I did not learn my workplace skills in Business School. Nor did I learn my workplace skills while working for a big corporation after college. I started learning my skills and getting career ready when I was 13. I have continued to use those skills for many years in many different businesses. They worked when I was 13, and they still work today. They will also work for you *if* you are lucky enough to learn the workplace skills early and then have a chance to practice them so that they can improve.

Start looking for your "Mr. Regan" as soon as possible. And remember, it could also be a Mrs. Regan! They aren't everywhere, but they are somewhere. There are many adults who are able and willing to go the extra mile to help you...if you are willing and able to ask for help.

What about Becky? Remember her? She was the only employee at the tennis store other than Mr. Regan and me. Becky is the person who changed my life and opened the door to success for me. She was about 27 years old when we worked together. She was twice as old as I was and not even half as old as Mr. Regan. But, for some strange reason, Becky thought she was a lot smarter than the rest of us.

It didn't take very long to find out that Becky wasn't nearly as smart as she thought she was.

Becky's main problem was that she thought she knew everything there was to know about business the day she starting working for Mr. Regan. So, when he tried to teach her the same workplace skills he was teaching me, she wasn't interested. She thought she knew it all already. Have you ever met someone like that? Some people look in the mirror and see someone like that. Don't be one of those people.

Back to Becky. She was actually my boss. When Mr. Regan was not in the store, Becky was in charge. She wasn't a very good boss. She was a little lazy, not very good with customers, often late for work, and mostly a pain in the you-know-what! Are you getting the impression that I wasn't a big fan of my boss Becky?

Get ready because I am not the only person in America who will have to deal with a difficult boss at some point. You will probably find yourself in the same situation sooner than later. Odds are pretty good that, eventually, you will have to deal with a boss who is a bit of a jerk. In fact, you might even have a boss who is more than a bit of a jerk. You might end up with a boss who is a total jerk!

It's not much fun when you don't care for your boss, but the experience doesn't have to be all bad. In fact, dealing with a difficult boss can also present some real opportunities in life.

The three years I spent working with Becky taught me a lot about dealing with difficult people. I learned that, no matter how unpleasant she was, I had to work through it and keep my eye on the prize. What prize? The prize was my *job,* and I didn't want to lose that prize just because my boss was a jerk. Working with Becky, day after day, gave me a chance to practice the skill of dealing with a difficult boss when I was just 13 and that experience has paid off ever since.

I know what you are thinking. How could I be going on and on telling you about my horrible boss Becky when just a few minutes ago I was telling you that Becky changed my life and that she opened the door to success for me? Doesn't make much sense does it? Hang on, it's about to make total sense.

Three years after I started working for Mr. Regan tragedy struck. It happened in an instant, and it was a total shock to everyone. Mr. Regan had a heart attack while playing tennis one day and dropped dead right there on the tennis court. No warning. No advance notice. His heart just stopped pumping, and he died instantly.

When Mr. Regan died I lost a great friend. Yes, teenagers can have friends who are much older. I also lost a great mentor. That man had taught me more about business in three years than I could ever have imagined. Finally, I lost the owner of the business where I worked. That's a lot to lose in one day when you are just 16 years old.

Mr. Regan's 40-year-old daughter took over the business and called a meeting with Becky to discuss the future of the store. The daughter knew nothing about the business and had to rely on Becky for answers to her questions. That was to be expected since Becky had been the store manager for some time. After their meeting, it was decided that the store would remain open. Becky would be the manager, and I would be the only other

29

employee (part-time). Remember, I was only 16 years old at the time.

So far, so good…until Becky tried to pull a fast one on the new owner.

After a few weeks Becky, who was now opening and closing the store every day, came up with an interesting idea. At the end of each day, for several days, Becky started trying on new clothes and shoes from the store right before closing time. She would take a stack of new clothes into the dressing room and come out of the dressing room wearing those new clothes. No big deal except that, for some reason, Becky somehow forgot to take off those new clothes and shoes at the end of the day and put her own clothes back on. Instead, she walked right out of the store, after closing for the day, wearing all the new clothes and shoes she had tried on. She then forgot to return those new clothes and shoes the next day or any day for that matter!

That's right, sweet little Becky was a full blown thief. Ripping off the new owner every chance she got. She was filling her closet at home with stacks of brand new clothes and shoes day after day. I started calling her Bad News Becky.

The whole scam worked pretty well until one day she left a bag filled with her old clothes at the store when she walked out wearing the new clothes. The new owner discovered the bag of old clothes the next day, confronted Bad News Becky, and proceeded to fire her right on the spot. My new name for her was Bye-Bye Becky!

The owner had all door locks at the store changed and called me in for a meeting the next day. I wasn't looking forward to that meeting. I was pretty sure the new owner was going to close the store or sell it since she knew nothing at all about running the business and she had just fired her only full-time employee, Bad News Becky. After school, I rode my bike to work just as I had done every other day. I walked into the store to meet with the owner, and that's when Becky changed my life and opened the door to success for me.

As you know, the new owner was Mr. Regan's daughter, so I had seen her often during the time I had worked for her father. She knew how much time her dad had spent teaching me about his business, and she knew what a great teacher he was. Mr. Regan's daughter asked me to sit down, looked right at me, and said, "How much do you know about this business?"

That's when my life changed. Right there at the tennis shop when I was 16 years old, I was about to find out just how career ready I really was.

I told Mr. Regan's daughter that I knew everything about the business, from start to finish, top to bottom. I explained that her dad had taken me under his wing when I was 13 and proceeded to teach me every aspect of the business. I thought she would be shocked, but she didn't seem surprised at all. She knew her dad, and she also knew how much he enjoyed sharing his knowledge and skills with young people like me.

Then, she blew me away with what she said next. She offered to pay me *five* times what I was currently being paid if I would teach her what I knew about the business that her dad had started, built, and left to her. I was stunned. That would be like someone offering you $40 an hour just to share what you know about your part-time job! I obviously accepted her offer, and as I walked out the store that day, all I could think about was how grateful I was that Bad News Becky was such a crook!

If Becky had not decided to *borrow* all those brand new clothes, she would have continued as store manager and no one would be interested in what some 16-year-old kid knew about the business. I love that Becky.

The workplace skills I learned as a teenager from Mr. Regan were all of a sudden the most valuable asset I had. I still use those skills today because they are totally transferable. That means I can take those skills from job to job and career to career for the rest of my life. This is important to me since I have already had eight or nine different careers, and I will probably have a few more before I'm done.

It will also be important to you much sooner than later.

<u>Notes</u>

Are You Interested?

Interested: Showing curiosity about something or someone.

As you have probably figured out by now, I have had the pleasure of meeting a great number of people over the course of my life. I suspect that I will continue to meet many more people for years to come. However, I don't think you can ever meet, get to know, *and* stay in touch with too many people.

The people I have met are a very diverse group. They come from all walks of life, which is probably what makes them so interesting to me. Since they come from so many different backgrounds, they all bring something different to the table. For that reason, they are all interesting in their own way. Because interesting people are not easy to find. I always enjoy my time with them when we cross paths.

The key to enjoying time with interesting people is all about your ability to ask questions. If you have learned and practiced questioning skills, you will *almost* be totally prepared to enjoy your time with interesting people, but to be fully prepared for the experience, you will also need great *listening* skills. Just remember the following:

1. Listening Skills must be learned.
2. Listening Skills can be learned at an early age.
3. Listening Skills only improve when they are practiced.

Sound familiar?

What makes some people more interesting than others? Let's face it. Some people are just a little bit dull and not particularly interesting. These are the people with whom you probably don't want to get stuck in a stalled elevator! These are also the people with whom you probably don't want to spend your 86,000 hours of work, right?

Remember all that *knowledge* we talked about earlier? The bits of wisdom you are being asked to acquire during your 20,000-hour educational journey? I'm talking about all that *stuff* your teachers want you to learn, but you aren't quite sure why you need to learn it. Well, this just might help you answer that "Why?" question.

The more of that *stuff* you learn, not just memorize, but learn, the more knowledge you will have at your disposal when the time comes to share your wisdom. Maybe it won't be in a stalled elevator, but I guarantee that you will have many opportunities to share your knowledge. The more you have to share, the more interesting you will be.

Why is it so important to be interesting? It's pretty simple. People like to be around other people who are interesting. And, employers like to hire employees who are interesting. And, most successful people are very interesting.

How interesting are you?

I have always believed that if you want to be a great *something*, like a great artist, a great teacher, a great basketball player, etc., you should try to find out what those great *somethings* have in common. What do most great teachers have in common? What do most great artists have in common? What do most great doctors have in common? I am always trying to figure out what the best of the best, in any arena, have in common.

Fortunately, that's the way it is with *interesting* people, too. If you want to be interesting, then you need to uncover the common denominators of interesting people. In my opinion, right at the top of the common denominator list for interesting people would be this statement: The most interesting people are usually those people who are also the most *interested*.

What in the world does that mean? In simple terms, it means that people who have an interest in a wide variety of subjects-- people, places, things, events, etc.--usually end up becoming some of the most interesting people out there. Their bucket of wisdom is not filled with all the same stuff. Their knowledge is diverse. Very few interesting people know everything about one subject, but they usually know a decent amount about a whole bunch of subjects.

How do they accomplish that? How do those people end up knowing a good bit about a whole bunch of subjects?

They *read* about it, and/or they *hear* about it, which brings us to what I believe is the most vital, critical, necessary, and useful workplace skill of all--the ability to communicate. You will never be career ready if you do not have good communication skills.

I don't live in a cave, so I am well aware that the art of conversation has evolved tremendously over the past several years. Very few conversations between teenagers are completed verbally these days. The transition to an environment where most communication has shifted to email, texting, tweeting, and blogging presents a huge opportunity for some of you.

Notice that I said the huge opportunity is there for *some* of you instead of saying *all* of you. That's because many of your classmates and friends will be moving so fast on the hi-tech train that they will totally miss the message that businesses around the world are sending to future prospective employees.

The companies for which you hope to work when you hit the real world are very clear in their desire to hire young people who can communicate with more than their thumbs. Don't misunderstand me here, and please don't be offended. There is absolutely nothing wrong with wireless communication. Text, tweet, blog, and email all you want. But, if you want to come out into the real world with a huge head start in the race to success, then be sure to develop a strong set of communication skills that involve more than two thumbs. The ability to communicate verbally (that would be with your mouth) is never going to go out of style. Most young people today have totally overlooked this fact, and that's why *you* have a huge opportunity here.

Think about it. What if you were on a plane, and suddenly, the pilot had a heart attack. Not just a mild heart attack but the real deal, and he dropped dead right there in the cockpit. The plane was flying 550 mph at an elevation of 30,000 feet. There was no co-pilot, and nobody on the plane knew how to fly…except you. You were the only passenger on the entire plane who possessed the skills needed to fly that plane. How valuable would you be at that point?

Or, what if you were at McDonald's one day having a quick lunch, minding your own business, when all of a sudden a five-year-old kid at the next table started choking on a piece of chewing gum? The kid's face was turning purple, and her eyes looked like they were rolling into the back of her head. The little girl's mom was screaming for help, begging for someone to save her child. Everyone in the restaurant was staring at the desperate little girl, but nobody could offer any help because none of them knew the skills of CPR…except you. How valuable do you think you might be then?

Having a skill that very few others possess will always put you in a position to take advantage of many opportunities. This will be particularly true when it comes to workplace skills. The way things are going, you will probably find yourself right in the middle of your own emergency situation when you hit the real world of work. Because most of your fellow teens will not figure this out, you have a chance to hit the world of work with a distinct advantage over the competition if you come out of the gates (i.e., school) with what will probably be the rare ability to communicate with your mouth as well as with your thumbs.

As you continue to recognize the value of technology, never underestimate the power of the spoken word--the ability of effective verbal communication. This will include good questioning skills and, just as important, listening skills.

If you have ever had a conversation with someone who was no more listening to you than flying to the moon, then you already know what I mean. The person with whom you are talking seems to care less about what you have to say. Individuals such as this are always interrupting you before you finish saying what you want to say. They often seem more interested in what *they* want to say next than what you are saying right then and there.

That is a perfect illustration of people who are not very interested. It might not be their fault that they are not interested people. Nobody is born interested in what others have to say. So, here we go again. The ability to be *interested* is yet another skill that will help you become career ready. And, since it is a skill, it must be learned and practiced.

Stick this little secret in your back pocket.

When you learn to talk to others about things that are of interest to them, two things will happen. First, you might well gain some wisdom that you did not have before, becoming more interesting in the process. Second, when you talk to others about subjects they enjoy, you will find that your relationship with them will grow much more quickly than when you show little or no interest in their jobs, families, and hobbies.

Here's a promise. Nothing will be more important in your career than relationships.

People make people successful. Write that down. Memorize it. Get it tattooed on your ankle. Do whatever you need to do so that you never forget it because that happens to be one bit of knowledge that is indeed relevant. No successful person anywhere in the world became successful without help from someone else.

That was the secret. Now, here's the advice.

Start practicing being the most *interested* person you can possibly be. Don't wait until you graduate from high school. Don't wait until next year or even next week. There is no better time to start than right now. The sooner you start, the more practice you will get, and the better off you will be. Just remember, there are other teens out there who are not waiting to get started on the career readiness race. Do you want them to have a head start?

On the subject of being interested, here is a bit of wisdom that has helped me a gazillion times (I know that's not a word!). When you know, in advance, that you will be meeting someone new, make it your business to learn a few things about that person before the meeting. Nothing is more impressive than someone who has taken the time to learn about my interests even before I meet them.

Before you go to a job interview, it is obviously a good idea to learn as much as possible about the company with which you are interviewing. That's always a good idea, but if you really want to succeed, you are going to need more than just *good* ideas. You are going to need a few *great* ideas. Here's one of those.

Before your interview, find out who you will be meeting. With technology today, it is usually possible to learn quite a bit about the people with whom you will be meeting prior to the interview. Do just that. Find out as much about them as possible. Learn what you can about their jobs, their families, their hobbies, and their interests, and then be ready to talk about all of it when you meet.

You will impress, you will surprise, and you will be remembered. Later on in the hiring process, when it comes down to making a final choice, that little extra homework you did might well be the difference between being hired and being *almost* hired.

Here's even better news.

The skill of being interested in others will serve you well as you look for a job. No doubt about it. That skill of being interested in others will also be incredibly valuable to you after you are hired. You will use this skill to develop strong relationships with your co-workers, and those close relationships with co-workers will determine how quickly you progress in your new position. Additionally, your co-workers can make life miserable for you, but they can also make things really sweet for you. Show them that you are sincerely interested in who they are and what they do. You will need their help at some point, and when you do need that help, the relationship must already be in place.

Speaking of needing help...I am the perfect example. I have never accomplished anything of any significance without the help of someone else.

As you may know, I spent eight amazing years as the host of my own television show which was seen on ESPN, the largest sports television network in the world. ESPN can now be seen in almost 100 million households. The show I hosted was called *Fly Fishing America,* and our crew traveled across the country each year in search of America's finest fly fishing destinations. We were able to go to some incredible places and meet many fascinating people as we filmed the *Fly Fishing America* episodes. A few weeks after we taped the shows, they would air on ESPN, and millions of people would get a chance to see, on television, what we got to see in person. It was truly an unbelievable experience.

At least once a week, somebody stops me and asks how in the world I was able to get my own television show on ESPN. Every time they ask, I spit out the same answer. I say, "It was actually pretty easy." Here's the story.

The year before I started hosting the show on ESPN, I was out in Utah fishing with a friend of mine. We all have friends, and they all have their own stories. In this case, my friend Brian was an actor, a pretty famous one at that time. To me, though, he was just another guy. Just like the rest of us. No big deal. He was just my friend, and we both enjoyed fishing.

In the midst of our fishing trip, I looked over at Brian and asked him what he had been doing lately (I was *interested*). Brian told me that he had recently returned from a great trip where he was a celebrity guest on one of the ESPN fishing shows. I asked him where they went, who went with them, and what they had done on the show. He told me all about the trip, the people, the process, and the places they fished.

When Brian finished telling me about his experience as a celebrity guest on the ESPN show, I told him that I would really love to do something like that one day. He immediately looked over at me with a smirk on his face and said, "Chad, you cannot be a celebrity guest on a TV show if you are not a celebrity, you moron!"

Since he was my friend, I ignored the whole moron reference and told him that my interest was not in being a celebrity guest but that I would love to host a show like the one on which he had been.

It sounded pretty cool to me. I loved to fish. I really enjoyed travel. The fishing show was a perfect combination of two of my passions. But, we're talking ESPN here, the largest sports television network in the world.

Anyway, that was the end of the conversation with my friend Brian, and we continued fishing until the sun went down. The next morning I flew back to Atlanta, GA, where I lived at the time and Brian flew back to Los Angeles, CA, where it would seem most celebrity guests live.

Six months later, I got a call from Brian.

At first I thought it was a joke he was playing on me, but when he wouldn't stop talking, I started to think it might be for real. Brian told me that he had just been back out on another ESPN show as a celebrity guest, and while he was there, he heard that they were about to get rid of the host of the show. Then, he suggested to the production team that they should call me about the *host* position.

I asked Brian why he had suggested me for the host position, and he reminded me that I seemed very *interested* in the show and the process when he first mentioned it to me six months earlier while we were fishing out in Utah. Then, he reminded me I had even told him that I would love to host such a show one day. Thankfully, he left out the whole moron thing this time around!

Believe it or not, the ESPN producer called about a week later and set up a meeting with me at the Atlanta airport to discuss the *Fly Fishing America* host position. I met the guy, John, in a small meeting room at the airport, and he proceeded to asked me at least 20 questions about all different aspects of fishing.

I answered every single one of his questions…apparently WRONG!

Then, he asked me if I had ever hosted a television show before. I said, "No, Sir." Next, he asked if I had ever been on a television series. I said, "No, Sir." Finally, with a look of disgust on his face, he asked me if I had ever been on TV for anything. For some reason, I decided to go with the truth and gave him one more straightforward, "Nope."

John, the producer, looked right at me and said, "You just don't have the experience we need for this position."

Then, before I could even respond, he added, "This show can be seen in 95 million households."

I started to say something, but he interrupted me to say, "You just aren't qualified to host this show."

That was enough for me, so I shook his hand, thanked him for meeting with me, and walked out of the room. What I really wanted to do was pour my cup of coffee right on his head, but since my cup was empty, that would not have worked very well.

Apparently, Mr. Big Shot producer walked out of our meeting and immediately called my friend Brian out in Los Angeles. Brian then called me to see what had happened in the meeting. I gave him the report; then, he told me that the producer had called him, all in a tizzy, and asked why in the world he had recommended me, Chad Foster, for the ESPN host job since I obviously had no television qualifications.

I asked Brian what he told the producer, and he said, "I told that producer that my friend Chad might not have any TV experience, but he can talk to a *stump*!"

Long story short…the ESPN production company was having a hard time finding a host for the show and finally decided to give me an opportunity to do a pilot for *Fly Fishing America*. A pilot is what they do for all shows to see if the network wants to put the show on TV full-time. It's just a single episode, so you only have one chance to get it right.

I agreed to do the pilot even though the producer told me I was only going to get to do the pilot because their plan was to go out and hire a *real* host as soon as possible. Needless to say, he did not have much faith in my ability to host the show.

I did do the pilot. ESPN did pick up the show for the full season. Mr. Big Shot Producer never did find his *real* host, so I had the great pleasure of hosting *Fly Fishing America*, seen in 95 million households, for the next eight years!

How did that happen?

Remember that day on the river in Utah when I showed a sincere *interest* in my friend Brian's experience as a celebrity guest on the ESPN show? Brian remembered my interest, so it was easy for him to think of me when he heard about the host opportunity on ESPN.

Did you get that? Let me say it one more time because it's really important.

The #1 reason why I was able to have my own television show on ESPN was the fact that I expressed my *interest* in what someone else was doing.

It's great to be interesting, but it's even better to be interested.

Look and Listen

As I am sitting here writing this book, it just occurred to me that I have no idea whether or not you are really interested in what I am writing. In fact, I have absolutely no clue whether or not you have any interest in what you are reading.

I find that a little strange. I mean here I am, sitting in a coffee shop, typing my little fingers off trying to convey a few things to you, the reader, yet I have no way of knowing if you are the least bit interested in what I have to say.

You aren't looking at me. At least I don't think you are looking at me. There is one young person sitting at a table near me who has looked my way a couple of times, but I'm pretty sure it's not you, right? I hope not because this guy seems to be a little weird.

And since you aren't here with me at the coffee shop, I guess it would stand to reason that, in addition to not looking at me, you are also not listening to me. You couldn't be listening to me since you aren't even here, correct?

You see, that's why I am totally sure that I have no idea whether or not you are interested in the information I am sharing with you. You aren't looking at me and you aren't listening to me.

I have a feeling I better make my point soon before you start thinking I need to be in therapy instead of in a coffee shop writing a book!

It is true that none of you are looking at me and none of you are listening to me. You couldn't be doing either because you are not here. But, what if you were here? What if you were sitting with me at the table in the coffee shop right now? If you were sitting at my table, and I was talking to you instead of typing, would I be able to determine your level of interest in what I am sharing with you?

Yes, I would. And it would not be difficult. It is all about eyes and ears.

If you are looking right at me while I am talking, I will believe that you are truly interested. If you are really listening to what I am saying, and not interrupting me mid-sentence, I will honestly believe that you have an interest in what I am saying. It's all about two simple words – *look* and *listen*.

This is true for every conversation you will ever have with anyone, anytime, anywhere.

An interested person is always a good listener. Good listeners are almost always good learners, and good learners always become very interesting.

Can you do it?

Notes

The $2 Million Dollar Mouth!

People Skills: The ability (skill) to deal with, influence, and communicate with other people.

Almost every time I speak at a school some bright (*interested*) student asks me why I decided to start writing books for teens. I love that question because it ultimately gives me a chance to tell all of my audiences just how stupid I really am.

Seriously, I wouldn't know how to walk out on stage and just start explaining what an idiot I am without a good leading question to get me started. I only need a little push to get me going on that subject; then, I can totally spill the beans.

I'm sure that none of you are stupid, and certainly not one of you is an idiot like me. But, that does not mean you and I don't have anything in common. In fact, I have something in common with every single one of you.

We have all made our share of mistakes. We have all messed up a few times, right?

Of course that's right, and it will continue to be right for the rest of our lives. You and I will continue to make mistakes (hopefully not the same ones), and we will mess up many, many more times before we take our last breath here on earth. That's just a fact of life. It's going to happen.

The real question isn't whether or not we will make more mistakes. The real question is what we will do after we make those mistakes, some of which will not be small mistakes. In fact, some of those mistakes will be big ones.

The bigger the mistake...the bigger the lesson...and the bigger the opportunity.

Write that down somewhere. Put it in a place where you can see it on a daily basis because that's how often you will need the advice. I got that advice when I was a teen, but I was too hard-headed to let it sink in and put it to use. Don't be like me.

Yes, we will all continue to make mistakes. You have been told a gazillion (still not a real word) times that you must learn from your mistakes. I have been told the same thing a bazillion (more than a gazillion) times, so I know how it feels.

I will assume that you know how to learn from your mistakes, so I won't go there. I am more interested in what you do with the knowledge you acquire through that learning process. Once you learn whatever it is you will learn from each mistake, what do you do with that wisdom?

I'm sure that wisdom will be helpful to you in the future. That's good news, but that's not great news. Great news would be finding a way for that wisdom to not only help you but also to help many other people at the same time.

That's why I write books and give speeches to teens across the country. I have made so many mistakes that you would need a calculator to keep up with the number. And yes, I have learned something from every mistake I have made, but that's not good enough for me. If I have learned something from a mistake I have made, be it a big one or a small one, then I have an

50

obligation to share what I have learned with others, be they young or old.

That's what else you and I have in common. We all have the same obligation to share what we learn from our mistakes.

You don't have to be old or famous or even successful in business to be qualified to share the lessons learned from your mistakes. If you are 17 years old, you have probably made plenty of mistakes already which only means that you have valuable wisdom to share. The question now is simple. With whom should you share that knowledge? Who is the best audience for your words of wisdom?

I would like to suggest that the valuable wisdom you have to share, as a result of your mistakes, will probably be better received by some audiences than it will be received by others. My guess is that audiences much younger than you will be most receptive to your valuable messages. I'll bet big bucks that if you walked into a 5th grade class one day and told those starry-eyed kids about a few of your dumbest mistakes, and the lessons learned from those mistakes, you would have them mesmerized by the time you walked out of that classroom.

How can that happen?

That can happen because you are what we call the right *messenger* for those 5th graders. The messages you deliver to that 5th grade class probably won't be new messages. In fact, they will probably be messages that most of us have heard many times. But, until those messages are delivered by the right messenger, they usually go in one ear and out the other. You have been there before, right? You have heard good messages in the past that were delivered by the wrong messenger and, therefore, were not successfully received. No big deal. We have all done it many times.

For some, you are the perfect messenger. If you are 14 years old, there is a 3rd grade class out there that is starving for your wisdom, but they probably don't want to hear it from their parents. From you, though, it might seem like great advice.

I have learned a few things from my mistakes along the way. A little earlier in this chapter I wrote a line that I asked you to remember for the rest of your life.

The bigger the mistake…the bigger the lesson…and the bigger the opportunity.

I didn't read that somewhere. Somebody told me that when I was a kid, but because I didn't listen, I had to figure it out on my own. Figuring things out on your own can be real painful sometimes.

Do you remember what my job was before I started writing books? That's right (I will assume you got it right)! I helped develop the soft, rubber playground surface you probably played on a few years ago at McDonald's.

Can you tell me the name of the surface that we developed? Right again. The surface is called SAF DEK, and we eventually installed our SAF DEK surface on more than 3,000 Playlands around the world. Just for your information, Playland is the official name of all McDonald's playgrounds.

Some people think that's pretty cool. In fact, some people even think I must be relatively smart to have done what I did. Those people are very mistaken. Read on, and you will soon see just how smart I am not.

I was just 27 years old when we developed the SAF DEK surface. I know that's a lot older than you, but it's really not very old in the business world. Most of the people with whom I was doing business were much older. That can make things tougher in some cases. Sometimes older business people won't give younger people a chance. That is unfortunate. Then again, sometimes younger people blow the chances they get. Stay tuned.

The McDonald's corporation is based in Oakbrook, IL, (hint: remember this) which is just outside of Chicago. That's where most of the McDonald's big shots work. The CEO, president, vice presidents, and many more big wigs have offices in Oakbrook. By the way, in case you were wondering...no, Ronald McDonald does not have an office there!

In addition to all the big shots, there are several thousand other people who work for the McDonald's corporation in Oakbrook, IL. There are people who work in the real estate division, the construction division, the training division, and even the product development division. That's where I spent most of my time – with the product development people – since I had introduced a new playground surface to the folks at McDonald's. So far...so good.

McDonald's is much like all huge corporations. Each division has a ton of employees, and each division also has one person who is definitely in charge. In the product development division at McDonald's, the guy in charge was Pat Hines. I was thinking about using a fake name for Mr. Hines, but since he no longer works for McDonald's, I decided to go with his real name. Besides, using his real name makes the end of the story even better.

Yes, Mr. Hines was definitely the guy in charge, and he reminded everyone of that fact as often as he possibly could. Mr. Hines (he did not want to be called by his first name) was really hard on his employees and spoke to them like they were morons most of the time. I would often get embarrassed when he started berating his fellow employees during meetings.

Mr. Hines was on a total power trip, which pretty much guaranteed that he was not going to be a big fan of mine, to say the least. Because I was not a McDonald's employee, Mr. Hines was not my boss...thank goodness. He did not like that at all.

From the day we met, Mr. Hines was determined to cause trouble for our little company. He did not like the fact that I was 27 years old. He did not like the fact that the new playground surface was our idea and not his. He did not like the price of our SAF DEK surface, and every time there was a problem on a job, Mr. Hines blamed it on us. Quite frankly, I don't think he much liked me...period. After a while, I started calling him Mr. Whines instead of Mr. Hines. Not to his face, of course!

Just to exert his power, Mr. Hines would have his assistant call me (he was too important to make the call himself) every few weeks, late in the afternoon, to tell me that Mr. Hines wanted to meet with me the very next day at 9:00 a.m. He knew good and well that to make it happen I would have to buy the most expensive plane ticket available since it was a last-minute trip. He also knew that I would have to cancel any and all meetings I had planned for the next day. None of that mattered to Mr. Hines because he was very important (at least in his own mind).

This situation went on for a few years until I just couldn't take it anymore. Another call from the assistant. Another request for a morning meeting the next day. Another rush to buy an expensive plane ticket and cancel all prior plans.

By this time, we had built more than 2,000 playgrounds for McDonald's. Our SAF DEK surface was extremely popular with the McDonald's franchisees across the country.

Meeting with Mr. Hines was the last thing I felt like doing, but I had no choice. Like it or not, he was in charge of new product development for all McDonald's restaurants, and they were our largest client, by far. In fact, the McDonald's account was 98% of our total business, and at that time, we were the only company they were using to install their Playland surfaces.

So I cancelled my plans for the next day, bought the horribly expensive plane ticket, and went to bed early.

It was bad enough that Mr. Hines always waited until the last minute to call these meetings but, even worse, he would never tell me what the silly meeting was going to be about until I walked into the meeting room. It was his way of making sure I had no time to prepare so that he would have every possible advantage. What a jerk.

I will never forget my meeting that next day with Mr. Hines. I walked into that fancy McDonald's conference room a few minutes early, and nobody was there. Just a great big table with eight massive chairs around it. I decided to sit at one end of the table since I knew Mr. Hines was going to be at the other end. He always sat at the end of the table. I think it made him feel even more important.

At 9:00 sharp, the conference room door swung open, and in they came, seven of them, all dressed up in their expensive designer suits and high-end Italian shoes. One by one, they walked past me, saying nothing as they went by, and took their seats at the table. As expected, Mr. Hines sat directly across from me at the other end of that great big table.

When Mr. Hines called a meeting, it always unfolded in the same manner. He would walk in without any pleasant greetings, sit at the head of the table, beat up on the product supplier (me), and then get up and walk out of the room. I expected this day to be no different.

The meeting probably would have proceeded just as expected…if only I had just kept my big, fat mouth shut. But, this day didn't quite go down that way.

Mr. Hines started the meeting by telling me that he had been doing some research. He went on to say that he now knew exactly how much it was costing our company to install the SAF DEK surfaces at the McDonald's Playlands. Finally, he looked right at me and said, "We know how much the rubber granules cost. We know how much the polyurethane binder costs. And, we know exactly how much your labor costs are."

Then, he paused, looked down at his file on the table, and finished by saying, "We know exactly how much all of your costs are, and you are charging us $22 per square foot for your SAF DEK surface. You guys are ripping us off!"

Right there! Right at that moment! That's when I had a chance to make an incredibly good decision. All I had to do was keep my mouth in a closed position for five minutes, and Pat the Rat (my other nickname for Mr. Hines) would finish beating up on me and walk out of the meeting, just like he had always done in the past.

Unfortunately, when I was in my 20s, I had a real hard time keeping my mouth in a closed position.

I looked up at Mr. Hines, took a deep breath, and calmly said, "Mr. Hines, with all due respect, as you know, I live in Atlanta, GA. As you also know, Atlanta is the corporate headquarters of Coke, which you serve at all McDonald's restaurants. As you might expect, I have several friends in Atlanta who work for Coke."

At that point, I started burning the biggest bridge of my life.

I looked across that great big table and said, "Mr. Hines, my friends who work at Coke have told me exactly how much you pay for the Coke syrup you use, and they also let me know exactly how much a large paper cup costs."

I stared right at Pat the Rat and said, "You guys are charging your customers $1.25 for a large Coke. Mr. Hines, you are the one doing the 'ripping off' around here."

Nobody flinched at that table. Not a sound came out of anyone's mouth. I'm sure those other six McDonald's employees had never heard anyone talk to Mr. Pat Hines that way.

It seemed like an hour, but I'm sure it was less than 10 seconds before Mr. Hines got up and walked out of that conference room without saying a word to anyone. The other six guys walked out right behind him and closed the door.

As I sat alone in that conference room, I remember feeling like I had just won the biggest fight of my life. I felt like I had just conquered the biggest, most powerful opponent I had ever faced. I had finally gotten the best of Mr. Pat the Rat Hines.

It was an amazing feeling.

It was also the dumbest thing I've ever done in my entire 35-year career. I went from relatively bright to absolutely stupid in a matter of 10 seconds.

Remember I told you that, at that time, we were the only company McDonald's was using to install their Playland surfaces. That was about to change as a result of Chad Foster's big, fat mouth that never should have opened.

Within 60 days, Pat the Rat Hines went out to California, set up a new company to compete against us, and gave the new company two hundred Playland projects to get them off to a great start. That's right, two hundred Playland projects at $10,000 per project. You can do the math. It makes me sick to my stomach to think about that number.

My big mouth and my oversized ego had just cost my company $2,000,000 dollars. In case you don't want to count those zeros, it comes to two million dollars!

The lesson here is simple.

Every one of you will eventually cross paths with your own Pat the Rat. That's a promise. The question is not *if* but *when*. You will have bosses and supervisors who are total jerks. You will probably have co-workers who are a pain in the rear. You might even have customers that treat you like dirt. It's all part of the real world experience.

The critical question is, "Will you be properly prepared to handle your Pat the Rat experiences? Will you be prepared to deal with the difficult people you will meet along the way?"

The ability to deal with difficult, unpleasant people is a skill. It is not something with which you are born or something that just comes to you at the last minute when you desperately need it. I proved that when I sat across the table from Mr. Hines. My inability to handle that situation properly cost our company two million dollars!

As hard as you work to do well in school in hopes of getting a great job in your chosen career, it might be interesting to note the following statistic. A recent study concluded that 70% of all people who lose or quit their jobs do so for one reason. Any idea what that reason might be?

Hint: It has nothing to do with money. It has nothing to do with work schedule. It has nothing to do with vacation days.

Are you ready?

This is valuable information, so please stick it in the part of your brain that doesn't leak. This little bit of career wisdom will serve you well for the rest of your life. Here it is.

Seventy percent (7 out of 10) of those people who lose or quit their jobs do so for one reason. They cannot get along with the people *for* whom they work and *with* whom they work.

If you ask me, that's incredible. In my opinion, that would make people skills some of the most important skills anyone could ever have.

These people losing and quitting jobs never learned the power of compromise. They didn't grasp the concept of win/win. And, most important, these people never understood the danger of burning bridges as they made their way through the real world of work.

I didn't lose my job, but I sure lost a bundle of cash for our little company--all because I wasn't totally prepared to deal with one difficult individual who turned around and made me pay, big time.

If you really want to be career ready, then make it a priority to learn and practice your people skills before a Pat the Rat walks into your life.

By the way, what would *you* do with an extra two million dollars?

<u>Notes</u>

You Just Never Know

Who have you met lately?

Seriously, can you think of a few people you've recently met...like in the past couple of weeks? If so, where did you meet these new people? Who are they? Will you ever see them again?

This is really none of my business. I was just wondering. Besides, what's the big deal about meeting new people anyway? You are just a teenager, right? Why would it be important for you to start meeting people at your age?

Those are all fair questions, so I'm glad you asked them. Now I will try to provide a few answers.

People are always asking me how I came up with the idea for the SAF DEK playground surface. It's not like I woke up one day and decided to develop a new product that McDonald's was going to buy for 3,000 of their Playlands. It just kind of evolved...sort of.

The first business I was in full-time after I completed my educational journey was a business that built tennis courts. I ended up in that business after a failed attempt at professional tennis during which time I travelled all over the world trying to make a living playing tennis. After 18 brutal months on the professional tennis tour, I had made a total of $425. That's right...a pitiful $425 in 18 months.

Let's face it. I was a total failure as a professional tennis player. Nevertheless, along the way, as I pursued that dream of mine, I met people all across the U.S. who played tennis, taught tennis, and even worked at tennis clubs. Those people I met as I pursued a dream, a dream that failed, helped me succeed in my first business venture. It was just one more reminder that people make people successful.

It was also a great example about the importance of pursuing your dreams, even the far-fetched ones. When you do that, sometimes the dreams do, in fact, come true...even the long shots. However, I have learned that even when those far-fetched dreams don't come true, as you pursue them other doors will open and other opportunities will present themselves. That's exactly what happened to me.

Soon after I got into the business, I built a tennis court for a man down in Louisiana. Let's just call him Mr. Ed for now. Anyway, I had never met Mr. Ed before we built his tennis court, but I got to know him pretty well over the course of the next few months. I was just 22 years old at the time, but I had learned from my dad many years earlier that I should stay in touch with everyone I met, if at all possible. So, I did just that. I stayed in touch with as many people as I could and that included Mr. Ed.

After we finished Mr. Ed's project, I started sending a short note to him every few months just to stay in touch and let him know what I was up to. Remember, Mr. Ed was a just a stranger before I did business with him.

Time out! Hold on! Pardon the interruption!

Did you see what just happened? I just tipped you off to how old I really am. Did you catch that hint? It was pretty obvious.

I just told you that I sent a short note to Mr. Ed every few months. I didn't say I sent an email to him every few months. And I didn't say I sent a text to him every few months, did I? So, how do you think I sent those notes to Mr. Ed?

Watch out. This might seem a little strange to many of you.

When I was ready to send a note to Mr. Ed, or any other business contact, I had to go to a store, buy a box of stationery, handwrite a note, fold the paper, slide it into an envelope, lick and seal the envelope, lick a stamp and place it on the envelope, and then put the envelope in the mailbox at the front of my house.

Can you believe it? Can you imagine having to do that much work just to get a short message to someone?

If you can't believe it, start believing. If you can't imagine that, start imagining. If you've never done it, start doing it.

Here's why.

As amazing as technology is and as convenient as it has made life for all of us, the number one tool in business today is the same as it was 20, 30, and even 50 years ago. The handwritten note is still king, and I suspect it will be for years to come. Nothing gets the attention of the recipient more than a handwritten note.

So, if you are thinking that I might be a bit older than you, you are definitely correct. But, that doesn't change the fact that a handwritten note will always be more powerful than an email, text, tweet, etc.

That does not mean you should discontinue emailing and texting. It simply means that, whenever possible, you should throw a handwritten note into the mix. It is and always will be a valuable tool.

Staying in touch with as many people as possible is known as networking, and when it comes to being career ready, the skill of networking is as important as any skill you will ever learn. The good news is that almost every one of you has darn-near perfected the art of networking on a social level. You do it practically every day, and you do it very well. All we need to do now is to help you transfer that skill to an arena that will assist you in your pursuit of professional success. I think it's an easy task, and I believe every one of you will be able to make it work, with some practice.

Back to Mr. Ed.

After a few years of building tennis courts, we expanded our little business and began to surface running tracks. We used a rubber surface for the tracks that was made from recycled tires. We mixed the rubber granules with a special polyurethane binder (glue) and paved the track surface much the same way you see the asphalt roads paved today. The result was a soft, durable track surface that was also porous enough for water to drain right through it after a rain. Needless to say, it was a very popular running track surface.

What does that have to do with Mr. Ed?

Well, in one of those short handwritten notes I sent to Mr. Ed, I mentioned that we were now in the business of surfacing running tracks with a new rubber surface made from recycled tires. I mentioned in my note that the new track surface had several unique qualities.

Bingo! Mr. Ed called me the day he received my note. He was wondering if I could drop off a sample of the running track surface for him to see. I agreed to bring a sample to his office the next day, all along assuming that he was thinking about building a jogging track in his huge backyard.

Once again, I was wrong.

When I walked into his office building, I was reminded of the business in which Mr. Ed was involved. There was a great big picture of a man named Ronald in the front lobby of the building. Can you guess what Ronald's last name might be?

That's right. Ronald's last name is McDonald, and Mr. Ed was a McDonald's franchisee.

Franchisees are the people who actually operate most of the McDonald's restaurants. They are entrepreneurs who buy one or more franchises from the McDonald's corporation; then, they run their own businesses. Most of the 32,737 McDonald's restaurants around the world are owned by franchisees. Only a small percentage of the McDonald's restaurants are actually owned by the McDonald's corporation. These are called company stores, and the McDonald's corporation uses these stores to test new products and procedures before they are introduced to the franchisee stores.

Mr. Ed explained to me that he, and all of the McDonald's franchisees, had a problem. They were in need of a new surface for their Playlands. He was wondering if we could use our new rubberized running track surface on a playground.

Before I answered his question, I asked him why he was looking for a new playground surface. He had an interesting answer to my question. He told me that McDonald's was currently using three different surfaces on their Playlands – bark chips, pea gravel, and sand.

"What is wrong with those surfaces?" I asked.

"Bark chips are the worst!" he said. "When it rains, the bark chips get soaked and anything that touches them after they are wet is instantly dirty. When kids play on our Playlands after even a short rain, their shoes and clothes get filthy dirty. Then, they walk into our stores and track all that dirt into the stores. Next, they get into their moms' cars and get them all dirty as well. Worst of all, when they get home, the dirt goes with them into their houses and the mothers go crazy. When they are finished going crazy, they still have to wash all those dirty clothes and clean the filthy floors."

I told Mr. Ed that bark chips did not seem to be a great idea; he agreed, reminding me that after every rain they have to close the Playlands for at least one day, sometimes more. That was costing the McDonald's owners a lot of money because parents will often not take their kids to McDonald's if the Playland is closed. Bottom line…no more bark chips.

Then, Mr. Ed said, "Pea gravel is no good either."

"Why?" I inquired.

Mr. Ed laughed and said, "Some kids pick up the pea gravel and throw those little rocks at the other kids. Sometimes the rocks miss the target and end up breaking one of the huge store windows."

So, no bark chips and no pea gravel.

There was only one more option, so I took a shot at it and asked, "What could possibly be wrong with sand as a Playland surface?"

Mr. Ed didn't hesitate. He looked at me with a dead serious face and said, "Chad, unfortunately, some little kids do the same thing in sand that cats do!"

I know. That's pretty gross, but apparently true.

I showed the sample of our rubber track surface to Mr. Ed, and he decided to give it a try. The rubber surface had never been used as a playground surface, so I simply made it a little thicker and a lot softer. Suddenly, we were in the playground business. No rocket science there.

The SAF DEK surface we developed was soft enough for kids to fall on without cracking open their heads. Like the running track surface, it was porous, so water would drain right through it immediately after a rain. Finally, it was extremely durable since it was originally developed to be used as a running track surface.

All we did was follow a simple formula for business that works in almost every career. We became aware of a need for a new product. We researched the existing products (sand, bark chips, and pea gravel). We addressed the weaknesses of the existing products; then, we assembled a team to develop, market, and install the new product.

Each stage of this process required a multitude of workplace skills. Without communication skills, people skills, networking skills, problem-solving skills, collaboration skills, and listening skills, we could not have pulled it off. Since we did not have hundreds of employees at the time, each of us had to make a multitude of contributions to the process.

I have a sneaky feeling that many of you will find yourselves in a similar situation sooner than later. My guess is that most of you will not go to work for a huge corporation when you complete your educational journey. If the current trend continues, and we have no reason to think it won't, the vast majority of you will work for smaller companies when you start your real-world journey.

In my opinion, this is great news for all of you. Working for a smaller company will provide many opportunities for you that a large corporation would not. You will likely be given more responsibility as well as more opportunities for advancement working for a smaller company.

If you really want to be ready for those opportunities and if you would like to have a sizeable head start in this real-world race, then now is the time to start loading your toolbox with all the skills that will provide substantial advantages for you.

Mr. Ed and his need for a new Playland surface was my window of opportunity. At some point, a window of opportunity will open for each of you. I can't tell you when or where your window will open, but I can tell you one thing for sure. If you are not *ready* when your window of opportunity opens, there is a good chance that the window will close. Even worse, there is absolutely also no guarantee that another window will open any time soon.

You already know the rest of the story, so I won't bore you with that. But, it is important to consider how I went from building one little tennis court for a total stranger to building 3,000 Playlands for the largest fast-food company in the world.

I have said it before and will say it many times in the future. People make people successful. And, it only takes one person to change your life, if it's the right person. That's why the more people you meet, get to know, and stay in touch with, the better your chances will be. You may have already met your "Mr. Ed" or you might meet him, or her, tomorrow.

Be ready. Be interested. Be real.

Meeting that person is only the first step in the networking process. Developing the relationship is next, and then you must stay in touch with everyone you meet.

Remember those short handwritten notes I sent to Mr. Ed? Had I not stayed in touch with Mr. Ed and kept him informed about our business ventures (a new running track surface), he never would have thought of me when he was in need of a new playground surface.

As I said, people make people successful. Notice that I did not say, "Only older people make younger people successful." Some people get a little confused about this. In fact, some young people think it is only possible for older people to help younger people.

Nothing could be further from the truth.

A few years ago, I was hired to give the commencement speech at a college in South Dakota. The commencement speech is the speech that is given at the graduation ceremony for colleges and universities.

At the South Dakota ceremony, there were several thousand people in the audience; thus, it was a pretty big crowd. It is also a big honor to give a commencement speech, so I was excited to be hired to speak at the event.

I flew to South Dakota from Atlanta and rented a car. I drove straight to my hotel and checked in. The next morning, I arrived at the civic center one hour before the ceremony was scheduled to start to be sure I had enough time to prepare to speak.

I learned that lesson a long time ago from my dad. He always said, "If an event starts at four o'clock and you arrive at the event right at four o'clock, then you are ten minutes late." I adopted that philosophy years ago, and it has served me quite well many times. Get there 10 minutes early, and you will always be right on time. Think about it.

At most events, there is not much to getting ready to speak, but when it's a commencement speech, the speaker usually has to wear a black gown just like the gowns worn by all of the graduates.

No big deal for most people, but I was having a heck of a time trying to get that silly gown on. For some reason, I could not find the pockets in the gown and was starting to think I might have it on inside out. What a knucklehead I was.

After fumbling around for a couple of minutes with that silly black gown, I heard someone behind me ask if I needed some help. Normally, that would be no big deal, but when I turned around to say yes, I realized that the guy offering to help me was actually the president of the college!

How embarrassing. This man was the person who actually hired me to give the commencement address at his college, and here I am not even able to get my stupid gown on straight. Needless to say, I felt like an absolute moron. I wanted to pull that gown up over my head and go hide in a closet somewhere.

As I was thanking the college president for his help, it occurred to me that the two of us had never met. So, I looked over at him and said, "Dr. Johnson, I don't believe that we have ever met, have we?"

Dr. Johnson said, "No, we have not met. In fact, I don't believe we have even spoken on the phone."

He was right about that. I had never spoken to the man in my life.

Then, I asked Dr. Johnson if he had received any information about me via email or even snail mail before deciding to hire me for this big commencement ceremony.

He assured me that he had never received any information about me via any kind of mail.

"Have you ever seen me give a speech?" I asked.

"Never," he responded.

At that point, I was getting a little confused. This man had never seen me speak, nor had he ever met me, yet he hired me to give the commencement address at his college's most prestigious event.

I couldn't resist. Even at the risk of further embarrassing myself, I just had to know. I turned to Dr. Johnson, president of the college, and said, "You and I have never met, and you have never even heard me speak. I am curious--why in the world did you decide to hire me to give this commencement address to your audience of several thousand people today?"

Dr. Johnson looked over at me and said, "Chad, the decision to hire you as our speaker was an easy one. South Dakota has a camp each summer for high school juniors called Youth Business Adventures."

Before he could say another word, I interrupted and said, "I know that camp. I have spoken at Youth Business Adventures every summer for the past five years."

Dr. Johnson looked back at me and said, "I know that already. You see, we have a 16-year-old daughter who attended the Youth Business Adventures camp this past summer. She spent an entire week there. The day she came home from camp she ran into our house, and even before she said hello to her mother, she walked up to me and said, 'Daddy, we had a great speaker at camp this week, and you need to hire him!' So I did just that."

Dr. Johnson did just what his 16-year-old daughter told him to do. He hired me, sight unseen, to give the commencement address at his college.

That 16-year-old helped *me* get that job. Sometimes it's a younger person that helps an older person out in the real world. You just never know.

The bottom line doesn't change. People make people successful.

As I sit here writing this book, there are 15 million people looking for jobs in this country. Unemployment has not been this high for several decades. Before you know it, you and your classmates will be in that group of people looking for jobs.

Some of those 15 million people who are currently unemployed will eventually find work. That's right. *Some* of those 15 million people will soon be employed.

On the other hand, most of those 15 million people will not find a job soon or maybe ever. They will remain on the unemployed list. There just aren't enough jobs to go around. There never will be. Those people who get stuck on the unemployed list will struggle, and they will suffer.

The real question is pretty obvious if you ask me. If there are not enough jobs to go around, then who will get the available jobs?

Will it be the smartest people on the unemployed list? Will it be the people who had the highest SAT scores or grade point average in high school?

I seriously doubt it.

I wholeheartedly believe that the majority of people who get the available jobs will be those people who know people who know other people who can help them.

Networking is a skill. That's great news because it means all of you can learn the skill, and all of you can improve your networking skills if you practice them. Now, it's pretty much up to you.

By the way, how many people do you already know who know other people who know even more people who can help you?

Notes

Are You Normal?

By the way, what color are your eyes? Do you think that is the normal color of a person's eyes?

And, while we are at it, what size shoe do you wear? Is that the normal shoe size?

Bear with me here. I am going somewhere with all of this, I promise.

If your eyes are blue, that's not normal. If it was normal, just about everyone would have blue eyes, but they don't, do they?

Likewise, brown eyes are not normal either, are they?

No, brown eyes are not normal and neither are blue eyes. And a size 8 shoe is no more normal than a size 7.

I could go on and on with this line of questions. I could ask about your skin color, height, weight, religion, age, gender, income, etc. I could fill the next five pages of this book with questions about what is and isn't normal. But I won't do that.

There is no need to ask any more questions because, at the end of the day, no matter how many questions I might have asked the bottom line won't change.

There is no normal.

That's right, there is absolutely no such thing as a normal skin color, religion, shoe size, weight, age, etc.

Understanding that concept, believing it, and practicing that belief are critical ingredients in the process of becoming career ready.

What's the connection between this whole *normal* thing and being career ready? Hang in there for a few minutes, and we'll try to make sense of it all.

I'm sure you don't do it anymore, but can you remember what it was like when, as a little kid, you used to play outside on the playgrounds? Like when you were three or four years old? If you can't remember that long ago, pay attention to the next playground you see as you are driving or riding around these next few days.

If you can remember your days on the playgrounds many years ago, think about what you saw out on those playgrounds. When you do, you will realize that not much has changed over the past 10-15 years since you were one of those little munchkins on the playground.

Playgrounds today are still filled with kids…kids from all walks of life. Tall kids, short kids; skinny kids, not so skinny kids; black kids, white kids; rich kids, poor kids. That's the way it was when you were hanging out on the playgrounds, and that's the way it was when I was out there, too. It has been that way for many, many years, and it probably won't be changing anytime soon.

Can you guess more specifically what kids will be doing next time you see a crowd of them on a playground?

That's right. They will be running, jumping, swinging, climbing, and playing...*together*.

Wait a minute. Why would all those kids be playing *together* when they are all so different? I mean some of them are short, some are black, some are rich, and some are skinny. How is it that they can seem to be so comfortable playing together when they are all so very different?

At the beginning of this chapter, we put the definition of a word in its own little box for you. That word is *tolerance*. Go back and check it out. You will see that the definition of the word tolerance is *the ability to recognize and respect differences that exist in others.*

The polar opposite of the word tolerance is the word *intolerance*, which would be defined as *the inability to recognize and respect differences that exist in others.*

What you are seeing out on the playground, as you observe all of those very different kids playing together, is a perfect example of tolerance, which is awesome. Those kids know good and well that they are different. It's not that hard to figure out. Some have white skin. Some have black skin. Some are Hispanic. Some of the kids have brand new clothes and shoes. Some of them are wearing clothes that don't fit and shoes with holes in them. Some of the moms drive fancy new cars while other moms drive old, worn out clunkers. Some of their dads are republicans and some are democrats. But, the 3-year-olds on the playground don't seem to care.

Why don't they care?

They don't care because 3-year-olds out on playgrounds all across America are not intolerant...*yet.*

Those 3-year-olds don't care what color skin the kid on the next swing might have. And they don't give a flip what kind of car their playmates' moms are driving. They truly don't care.

Why did I say that the 3-year-olds are not intolerant *yet*?

I said it because it's true. This goes back to the whole "tell the truth, the whole truth, and nothing but the truth" thing. Virtually, no 3-year-old is intolerant, a small percentage of 5-year-olds are intolerant, and quite a few 8-year-olds are intolerant.

After that, the flood gates open, and intolerance can be seen all over the place. By the time most people are adults, intolerance is just a way of life. Fortunately, there is a very simple explanation for that phenomenon. And, even more fortunate, the trend can be reversed by people like you.

Intolerance is a learned behavior.

Nobody is born intolerant, and nobody is forced to live a life of intolerance. It is a choice that we all have to make on a daily basis as we navigate our personal and professional journeys. As we get older, it is extremely important for all of us to understand the poison of intolerance. It is equally important to understand that intolerance can cause you to crash and burn when you hit the real world of work.

By the way, I am incredibly intolerant at times.

No kidding. I am guilty of demonstrating horrible intolerance on a fairly regular basis. I have been doing it for years, and I can't seem to stop. I have absolutely zero tolerance for people who smoke.

In my mind, I know it is none of my business if someone else wants to smoke, but I still struggle with smokers more often than I would like to admit. I can't stand the smell of cigarette smoke. I don't like how my clothes smell after being in a room with someone who is smoking. I am just down right intolerant of smokers, and I have been that way for a long time.

I need to change my behavior.

For me, it's smokers. For others, intolerance might be about race, religion, gender, or physical appearance. The truth is, almost every one of us is intolerant in some way.

We all have to change our behavior before the poison of intolerance takes its toll. You will have a major advantage in the world of work if you can walk into the real world loaded with tolerance. On the other hand, if you carry the poison of intolerance with you into the workplace, your chances of success are slim to zippo!

This is no easy task. Remember, intolerance is a learned behavior and just about every one of us has learned it to some degree. Breaking the cycle of intolerance is tough, and it doesn't happen overnight.

Just stop for a minute and diagnose yourself. In what area or areas are you intolerant? If you don't think you are intolerant at all, I suggest that you get up and take a look in the mirror. You might be able to fool all of the people some of the time and some people all of the time, but you can't fool the face in the mirror. No way will you ever be able to fool yourself. There is nothing wrong with admitting a character flaw. You can't correct a shortcoming until you admit the shortcoming exists.

Here's a little secret I learned a long time ago about intolerance. As our definition of *intolerance* states, this behavior is all about differences. Someone looks different, has different beliefs, acts different, dresses different, etc.

Wait a minute! Hold on! Time out! It is happening right now. A guy just walked into the coffee shop and sat down at the table next to me. He totally reeks of smoke. He is sitting five feet away from me, and this whole section of the coffee shop is already starting to smell like cigarette smoke. Can you believe it? He didn't even light up and the whole section stinks.

What do you think I should I do?

Don't answer that question just yet.

Last year I was in Texas giving a speech to about 400 teachers from all across the state. Before I started speaking, I posted a sign in all four corners of the room. On each sign, I wrote the name of a specific vehicle. One sign read Ford F-150 Pickup, one read BMW Convertible, one read Volkswagen Beetle, and the last sign read Harley Davidson Motorcycle.

In the middle of my speech, I stopped and asked the audience, all 400 of them, to look at the signs posted in the four corners of the room. I then asked everyone in attendance to get up from their seats, as quickly as possible, and walk straight to the corner that had a sign representing the vehicle that they would most prefer to drive, based on the four choices provided.

The place went crazy. Just imagine 400 teachers, all jumping up at the same time, trying to get to their chosen corner as quickly as possible. People were running into each other, left and right. You would have thought we were giving away the vehicles to the person who reached the corner first!

I had done this a few times before, so I thought I knew what to expect. Little did I know that I was about to discover one secret to curing the poison of intolerance.

As the 400 teachers zigged and zagged their way across the room, I saw something I will never forget. As you know, the vast majority of teachers are female. Not to generalize, but you can probably guess in which direction most of the women were headed. That's right. The women were just about equally split between the Volkswagen Beetle corner and the BMW Convertible corner. A few of them were making their way over to the Ford F-150 corner. Just as expected.

Then, it happened. Right there in front of me.

I saw an older black woman, probably in her late 60s, slowly making her way through the crowd in what looked to be the direction of the Harley Davidson Motorcycle corner. Then, out of the corner of my eye, I saw another woman heading in the same direction from the opposite end of the room. This lady was white and looked to be in her mid-20s. I assumed that she was a newbie teacher. The crowd was starting to thin a bit, and as it did, these two teachers looked at each other and realized that they were both headed in the same direction – Harley Davidson.

At that very moment, both teachers began to smile. They were getting closer and closer to the Harley Davidson corner where there were at least 60 men standing, all huddled together. Not a single woman was in the group...yet.

By the way these two women were looking at each other, I could tell that they didn't know each other, but their smiles were getting bigger by the second. It was like the two women had some kind of magnets in their pockets as they approached the Harley Davidson corner. They arrived at the corner of the room at just about the same time and immediately started talking to each other.

Once all 400 teachers had reached their respective corners I was ready to continue my presentation. As I was about to start, I looked back over at the Harley Davidson corner and saw the two women still talking to each other, paying absolutely no attention to me. Then, I saw the two of them exchanging some kind of written information as they continued their conversation. I really needed to get on with the show, but for some reason, I couldn't get these two women to shut-up!

How could this be happening? How could these two women be getting along so well after being together less than two minutes? Especially since they were obviously so different. One of the teachers was in her sixties and had black skin while the other one was a white woman in her twenties. They didn't teach at the same school and didn't even live in the same town.

These two women could not have been more different, but these two teachers were not focused on their differences. They were one hundred percent, totally focused on one similarity... motorcycles! The two very different teachers were standing in the middle of that room, completely ignoring the speaker, exchanging contact information so that they could meet to ride their motorcycles together some day!

That's right. These two very different individuals were quickly developing a relationship based on one simple similarity-- motorcycles, in this case. They weren't focused on the fact that they had different color skin or the fact that they were generations apart in age. They were only focused on that one similarity.

On this day, it was motorcycles, but it could be anything. It could be family, career, hobbies, etc. That is the secret to *unlearning* the behavior of intolerance. Always focus on similarities – not differences.

If you will always make a point to focus on similarities instead of differences when you cross paths with others unlike yourself, you will have an opportunity to develop relationships with people from all walks of life... relationships that you might enjoy for the rest of your life. Some of those relationships might be social, and some will prove to be professional.

The entire relationship can easily be built based on just *one* similarity, but if you are too focused on your differences, you might completely miss the similarity. Remember the Harley Davidson girls?

Intolerance is a learned behavior, and it can be unlearned. In fact, it *must* be unlearned.

I have the honor of giving more than 100 speeches each year to audiences across the country. In fact, 75% of my annual income comes from speaking. It is not important how much money I make from speaking, but it is important to understand that speaking brings in 75% of my total income each year.

Why is that important to know?

By itself it is of little importance, but when you add one other number to the equation, it becomes incredibly important. In fact, it becomes pretty darn scary.

The next number to be added to the equation is 90%. That number represents the percentage of times I get hired by a female to give a speech. Are you with me here? Of the 120 speeches I am hired to give each year, 90% of the time it is a woman who hires me. That means 108 times each year some female somewhere in America is in charge of deciding whether to hire me as the speaker or to hire somebody else.

Earlier in this chapter, I mentioned several areas in which some people might be intolerant. One of those areas is *gender*, which means male or female. Some people are intolerant when it comes to working with someone from the opposite gender. Believe it or not, some women have a hard time working with men, and likewise, some men have a difficult time working with women.

What if I was one of those people? What if I was like some people who have a hard time working with women? What would happen to my speaking business if I was intolerant of females? I could kiss 90% of my business good-bye. The fact of the matter is that I would pretty much be out of business if I had a problem working with women. That is a perfect example of how the poison of intolerance can destroy careers.

When people are trying to decide which speaker to hire, they have to make a choice, and there are hundreds of people from whom to choose. I am not the only speaker on earth, and I can assure you that no woman is going to hire a speaker who has a reputation of being intolerant of females.

Intolerance can be very costly in the world of work.

Here's why you will have an advantage if you make tolerance a priority in your life.

In an earlier chapter, we talked about the importance of pursuing your passion(s) as you work toward being career ready. We also discussed the fact that just about every one of you will have 7-8 careers over the course of your lives. And, we also reminded you that the majority of your generation will probably work for smaller companies rather than huge corporations.

As you move from career to career and even job to job, we know one thing for sure. You will have to work with other people every step of the way. The number of people with whom you will work will vary from job to job. In some cases, you will be working with a large number of people, and in others, the number will be smaller.

The people with whom you will work are composed of three primary groups. One group will be known as your supervisors. These are the people to whom you will report and answer. They are your bosses and the bosses of your bosses. I usually call those people the *big* bosses.

A second group will be your co-workers. These are the other people who work for the same company. Some of your co-workers will work in the same office as you while some might not even live in the same town.

The final group of people with whom you will work is made up of your customers. Whether you are in sales or not, you will more than likely have to interact with your company's customers on a regular basis.

Even if you do work for a small company, the total number of people with whom you will have contact is going to be substantial. If you add up all of the supervisors, co-workers, and customers at your place of work, you will be talking about quite a few people. For those of you who have worked or are working part-time, you already have an idea how many people we are talking about here.

At some of the companies where you will work, the number of supervisors, co-workers, and customers could be in the hundreds or even higher. Then, if you do change careers 7-8 times, like current studies predict, you can multiply that number of supervisors, co-workers, and customers by seven or even eight. That will give you a pretty good indication of how many different people with whom you will come into contact over the course of your 86,000-hour working life. We could be talking about thousands of people!

What do you know about all those people? Do you know anything at all about them?

I have no idea where any of you will eventually work, and I definitely have no idea with whom you will work. But, I do know that when it comes to your supervisors, co-workers, and customers, 99% of all workers, including you, will have something in common.

1. **You will not be able to choose your supervisors (bosses).**
2. **You will not be able to choose your co-workers.**
3. **You will not be able to choose your customers.**

That's right. It is going to be totally out of your control when it comes to *for* whom you work, *with* whom you work, and who your customers might be. It will be that way at your first job, and for most of you, that will be the case with every job you ever have.

Here's another secret to save in the part of your brain that doesn't leak.

Since 99% of you will not be able to choose your own bosses, co-workers, and/or customers, it is going to be vitally important that you walk into every work environment you ever encounter full of tolerance for anybody and everyone with whom you cross paths. If you enter the workplace as an *intolerant* employee, you will struggle and you will not succeed.

Your future bosses could be Hispanic, White, African American, Asian, or Native American. You just never know, and it's totally out of your control. Do any of those possibilities cause concern for you? At some point you could have co-workers who are Muslim, Catholic, Jewish, Baptist, etc. Is that going to be a problem? You might even have a customer who is 200 pounds overweight and sweats like a pig. Are you okay with that? There is absolutely nothing wrong with any of the people I just described. They just might be very different from you, and that's where you will need a double dose of tolerance, if you want to be successful.

Bottom line…you will not be able to choose your bosses, co-workers, or customers, so you must enter the world of work tolerant of all people. You are lucky because you still have time to unlearn any intolerance you may have learned as a younger person. Remember, you are not alone. We all learned some degree of intolerance along the way, and we all have the ability to unlearn it as well.

Beware. You may live in a house with parents and/or siblings who are very intolerant. You will probably have friends and classmates who are intolerant as well. This might make the process of unlearning intolerance a little bit more difficult for you. Please do it anyway.

<u>Notes</u>

FYI...

Now that I just wrote almost 24,000 words trying to tell you what it will take to get career ready, I have some news for you that might be surprising.

No matter how hard you work to get career ready before you enter the real world of work, you will still never love 100% of your job.

That does not mean you won't love the vast majority of what your job includes. It simply means that, with all jobs, there will be certain aspects of the job you don't particularly enjoy, and that's okay. If you understand this on the front end, it won't be a big deal.

I love what I do for work. I truly enjoy writing books and speaking to audiences around the country. However, there are parts of the job that I just can't stand.

When I am booked to speak out of state, I have to leave for the airport three hours before my scheduled flight time and then drive in the ridiculous Atlanta traffic for at least an hour--longer if there is a wreck on the interstate. When I arrive at the airport, I usually have to eat some of their over-priced, less-than-delicious food and then rush to my gate where I will sit amongst hundreds of people breathing germ-filled air. When I finally get on my flight, which is often delayed, I have to sit in a cramped seat for hours next to someone who may or may not have bathed that day. If my seatmate decides to take a snooze, the odds are pretty good that he or she will soon be snoring right in my ear or maybe even drooling on my shoulder! When the plane lands, we will all be herded to the front like cattle as we make our way to the terminal where we will have the great pleasure of waiting another 15-20 minutes for our luggage to be delivered, unless it gets lost in transit. All I have to do now is stand in line at the rental car counter for 10 more minutes just so that I can walk outside and get on the rental car bus that will take me to the rental car lot where my rental car may or may not be ready. Now I get to drive on unfamiliar roads for some period of time, possibly in a rain storm, until I reach my hotel. Once there, I will stand in yet another line waiting to check into my room where a very uncomfortable bed will probably be waiting. Ouch!

Did I mention that there are parts of my job I really can't stand? Let me be totally honest. I hate the traveling part of my job.

But, after all that miserable traveling, I get to stand in front of a bunch of talented, bright students like you and share the lessons I have learned through my own personal successes and failures. For me, that is extremely rewarding. I also get a chance to meet lots of strangers and make many new contacts every time I arrive in a new town or city. I enjoy that a great deal. Then, after I get back home, I have the pleasure of hearing from readers like you and your classmates who kindly provide feedback about my books and speeches. This is always a real pleasure. You see, there are many, many aspects of my job that I truly do love.

It can work that way for you as well…if you are *career ready* when you arrive.

Good luck. Get ready. Work hard. Have fun.

"Career Ready" Recipe

Ingredient #1 – Character
Who you are and what you do when nobody is looking.

Ingredient #2 – Productivity
The amount of work that comes from a given input.

Ingredient #3 – Attendance
The act of being present.

Ingredient #4 - Respect
Valuing another person's point of view.

Ingredient #5 - Teamwork
The process of working together with a group of people.

Ingredient #6 - Cooperation
Working together in a positive manner for a common purpose.

Ingredient #7 - Communication
The imparting or exchanging of information.

Ingredient #8 - Attitude
Responding positively or negatively towards a
certain idea, object, person, or situation.

Ingredient #9 – Tolerance
The ability to recognize and respect differences that exist in others.

Ingredient #10 – Commitment
The act of pledging oneself to an idea, cause, or action.

This Book Was Read By:

Name	Start Date	Finish Date
1. _____	_____	_____
2. _____	_____	_____
3. _____	_____	_____
4. _____	_____	_____
5. _____	_____	_____
6. _____	_____	_____
7. _____	_____	_____
8. _____	_____	_____
9. _____	_____	_____
10. _____	_____	_____

Notes

Notes

Notes

<u>Notes</u>